AN EARLY CRAFT BOOK

PRINT MAKING

by SUELLEN MacSTRAVIC *pictures by* G. OVERLIE

Lerner Publications Company • Minneapolis, Minnesota

J
761
M

LIBRARY OF CONGRESS CATALOGING IN PUBLICATION DATA

MacStravic, Suellen.
Print making.

(An Early Craft Book)
SUMMARY: Explains how to make prints from fruit, vegetable, fabric, and wood blocks and gives suggestions for independent projects.

1. Prints—Technique—Juvenile literature. [1. Prints—Technique. 2. Handicraft] I. Overlie, George, illus. II. Title.

NE860.M24   761   72-13344
ISBN 0-8225-0859-1

Copyright © 1973 by Lerner Publications Company
ISBN No. 0-8225-0859-1
Library of Congress No. 72-13344
Printed in U.S.A.
Second Printing 1974

Contents

A long time ago 5
Your first prints 8
    Tools and materials 9
Printing with blocks 20
    Tools and materials 22
A bean block 24
A fabric block 28
A wood block 28
Other projects 30

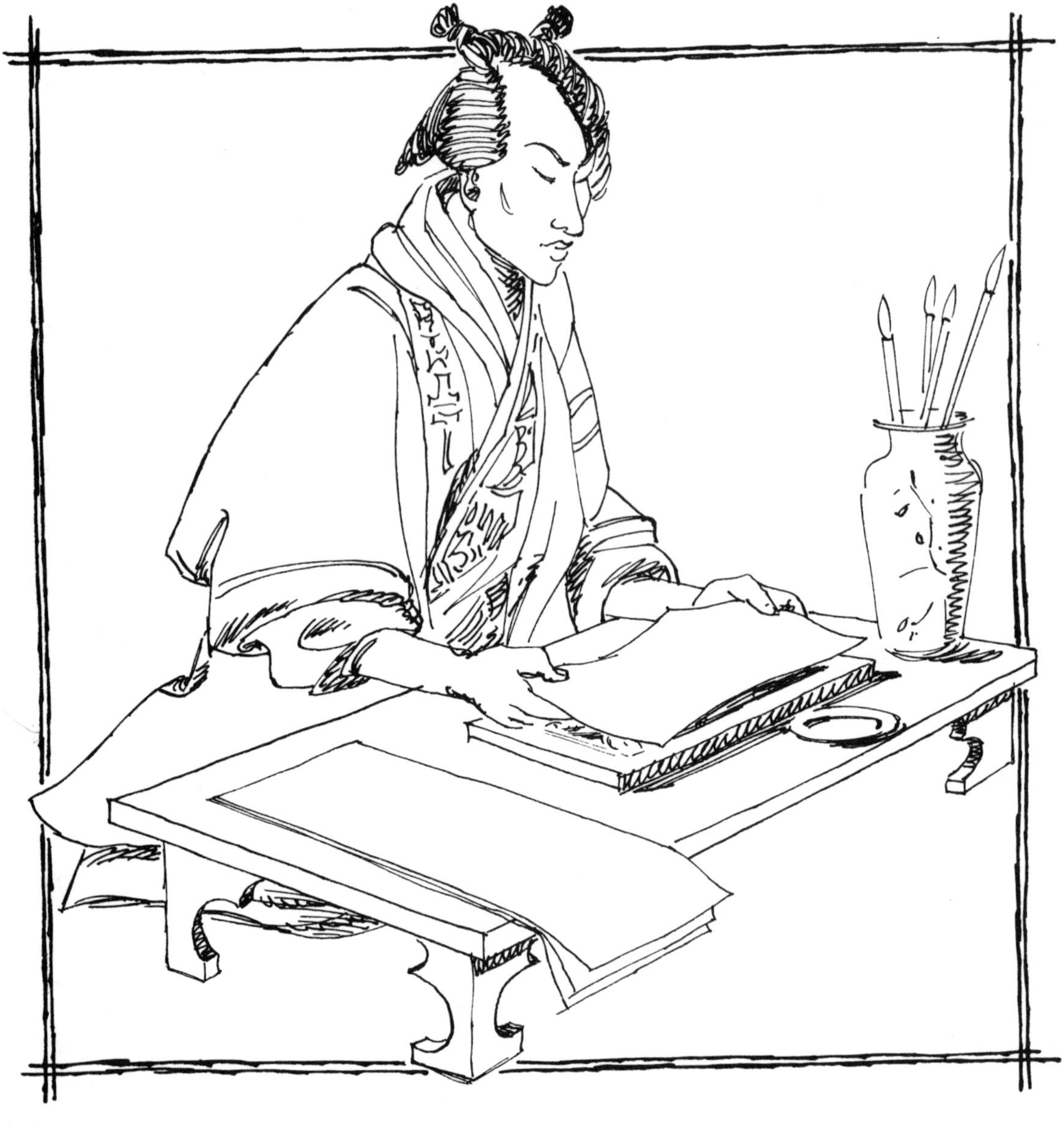

A long time ago

Whenever you mark an object like paper or cloth with pencil, ink, or color, you are "printing" on that object. A printing machine, or press, made the marks—the letters and pictures—on this page. They have been copied thousands of times to make many books just like this one. It would have taken a long time to make the copies if someone had written the words and drawn the pictures by hand.

The first people to invent printing were the Chinese. They invented it almost immediately after they invented paper more than two thousand years ago. The Chinese printed words and pictures with wooden blocks.

About 1,500 years later, a man from Germany, Johannes Guttenberg (yo-HON-us GOOT-en-berg), made the first printing press. It was a marvelous machine. Because it could print many books, all children, rich and poor, could read and learn.

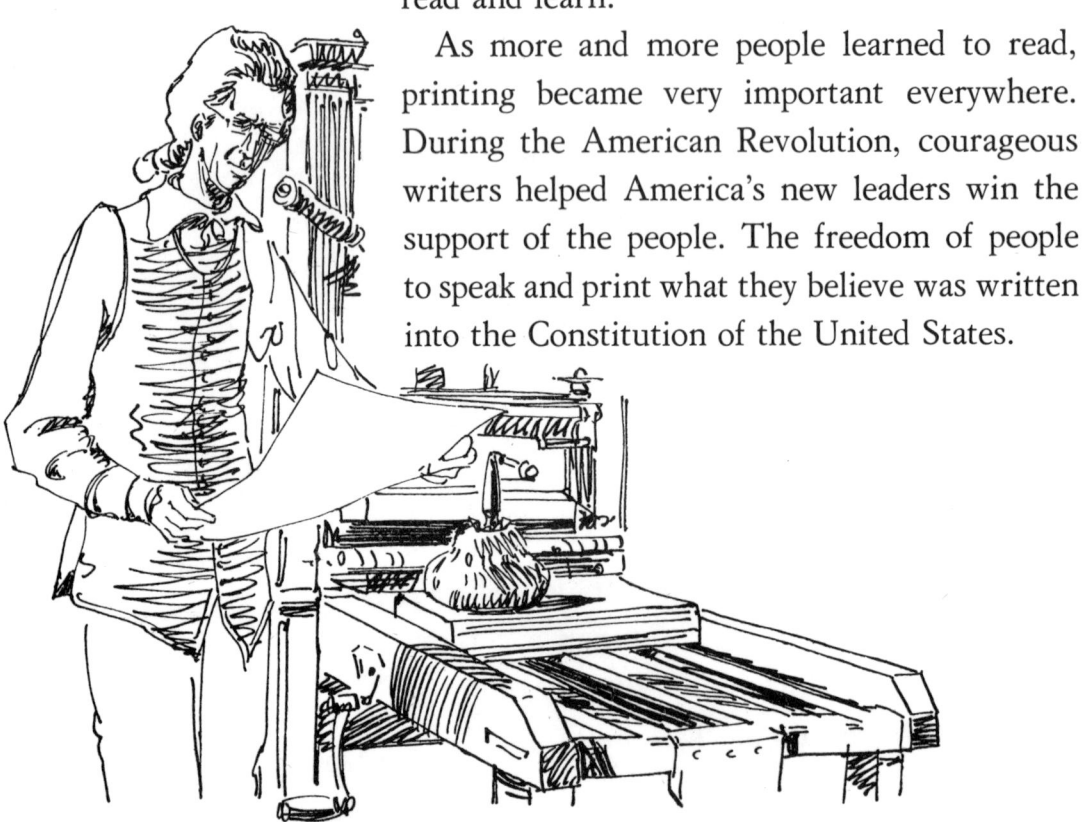

As more and more people learned to read, printing became very important everywhere. During the American Revolution, courageous writers helped America's new leaders win the support of the people. The freedom of people to speak and print what they believe was written into the Constitution of the United States.

As this country grew, printed material became common in every household. People read books and newspapers and hung printed pictures on their walls. They sold their goods through printed advertisements. They put up "wanted posters" to catch outlaws.

We cannot work with a printing press to print books or advertisements. Presses are large machines and people must be specially trained to work with them. But we *can* work with the principle of printing. Would you like to learn how?

You can print designs and pictures, and you can make as many copies of the same design as you like. You can use your prints in many ways. You can, of course, hang them on your wall. You can also use them for wrapping paper, greeting cards, posters, or party placemats for the table. You can use them in as many ways as you use paper.

Your first prints

Your first prints will be made in the same way that the ancient Chinese printed words and pictures. You will press objects that are coated with paint onto a piece of paper. The process is interesting, because some of the objects will make very surprising designs. Your prints will look very different from the pictures you usually draw or paint.

Tools and materials

Before you can begin to make your prints, you must collect the materials you will need. You should have:

>a small can of condensed milk
>
>liquid tempera or poster paint in several colors
>
>several old glass or china plates or pie tins
>
>a package of paper napkins
>
>12 sheets of newspaper
>
>paper towels
>
>fruits and vegetables to print with
>
>newsprint or construction paper to print on.

You can buy the paints and paper at any hobby or art store.

Fruit and vegetable prints are good to start with. If you look at some famous paintings, you will see that artists have always liked to paint natural things. They have painted pictures of bowls of fruit and flowers, pictures of the sea and beach, and beautiful landscapes with trees and mountains. By making fruit and vegetable prints, you will also be using natural things in art. You will see how artists and craftsmen imitate and use natural designs. For example, how is a cave like a house? How is a log like a wheel? Why is a sunset beautiful? There is so much color and design in nature. You will see some of it in your first prints.

You will make your first prints with fruits and vegetables that have been cut in half. You can use a cucumber, a mushroom, a green pepper, an onion, an orange, or an apple. I like them all.

First you must cut the vegetables and fruits in half across the middle. Let them dry in the air thoroughly. If they are dry, they will make clearer prints. Cut a green pepper in half. You will see that the inside has a lovely design. Cut an orange in half. See how the segments of the orange form a design? Let's make some prints with the green pepper and the orange.

cut a green pepper and an orange in half

You must begin by making an "ink pad" out of the paint. If you want your print to be made with two or three colors, you must have that many ink pads.

You might want to use a green ink pad and an orange ink pad if you are going to print with the pepper and the orange. You can use any color you like. The print you make might be more interesting if you use surprising colors.

To make an ink pad, place six of the paper napkins on a plate or pie tin. Then mix 1/4 cup of canned milk and 1/4 cup of poster paint together. Pour the milk and paint mixture over the napkins in the dish. Let the mixture soak into the napkins for about 10 minutes.

¼ cup condensed milk • ¼ cup poster paint

six napkins   *plate or pie tin*

While the paint is soaking into the napkins, you can prepare your printing surface. First, spread the table you are working on with layers of the newspapers. The newspapers will cushion your printing surface. Prints are always clearer and sharper when the surface "gives" under the pressure of the "block." If the surface was very hard, the paint or ink would smear and the print would look smudged. The newspapers will also keep the table clean. Put a layer of paper towels on top of the newspapers. Now you can select the paper you want to print on.

layer of paper towels

layer of newspapers

Take a sheet of newsprint or a sheet of construction paper and place it on top of the paper towels. By this time, the ink pads will be ready and the fruits and vegetables will be dry. You can begin to print.

Let's print with the orange first. Press the flat side of the orange onto the ink pad. Lift it up and press it lightly on the paper. Then carefully take it off the paper. What a pretty design! Did you know it was going to look like that?

print from an orange

You can press the orange onto the ink pad and then onto the paper many times. You can fill the page with orange designs. Then try the green pepper and make a page of green pepper designs. Design a page using both the green pepper and the orange. Ink and press all of the different fruits and vegetables you have at hand. Use your imagination. Use as many colors as you like.

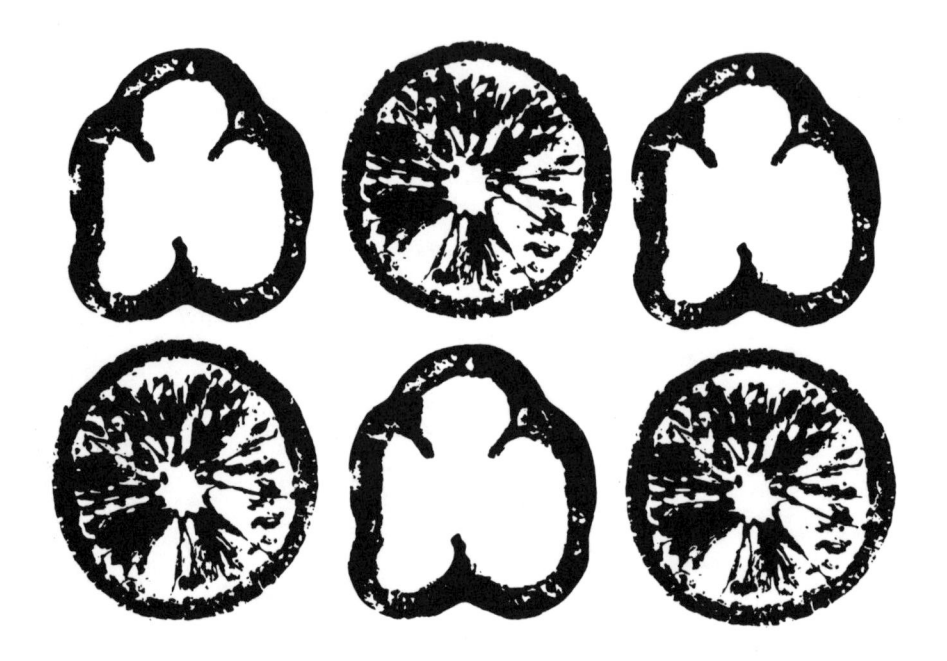

17

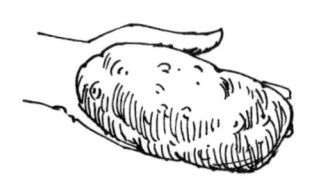

slice off sides and ends

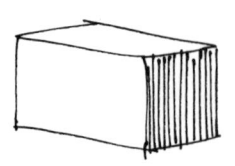

draw design

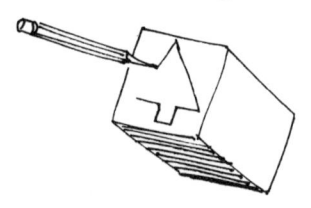

carve design

You can print with a potato in a special way. Because it is easy to carve a design from a potato, you can add a personal creative touch to the prints you make from other fruits and vegetables.

To make a potato block, choose a small potato that fits nicely in your hand. Slice off the sides and ends of the potato. Then carve a design in one of the ends of the block. Make a simple design like a pine tree or a tulip. First, draw an outline of the design on the block with a pencil. Carve the potato away from the edges of your drawing. The outline of the pine tree, for example, should be raised from the surface of the block.

Dry the block with a paper towel, and print with it as you did with the other vegetables. Add potato block designs to other vegetable designs to make a print with many different shapes.

dry with paper towels and print

There are many other objects that will make pretty prints. Look out-of-doors. Fresh leaves make beautiful prints. Press them onto the ink pad and then onto your paper. You can also use rough bark, pine cones, sea shells, seed pods, and bumpy pebbles to make prints.

Look around your house for objects to print with. You can use anything that will not be hurt by poster paint. If the object can be washed or thrown away, you can use it. You can print with sandpaper, small squares of burlap cloth, bottle tops, keys, sponges, a potato masher, or anything you find that will make a pretty design.

You might want to print an entire sheet of paper with a sponge and let it dry. Then you can print other objects on top of the paper that has been "textured" with the sponge.

brayer

wooden spoon

Printing with blocks

When you have learned to make simple prints like the fruit and vegetable prints, you can begin to make prints with printing "blocks" or "plates." These blocks will be like the potato block, but they will be larger and you will be able to make designs that have more variety.

We will work with two kinds of blocks. Both begin with flat surfaces, but one will have objects glued onto it and the other will have designs scratched or carved into it. When you glue objects onto the flat surface, only the design you make with the objects will print. When you scratch or carve designs into a flat surface, only the raised or uncut surface will print. For example, if you print with blue ink on white paper, the background of the print will be blue and the design will be white. The ink does not sink into the design. It covers only the uncut surface.

cardboard

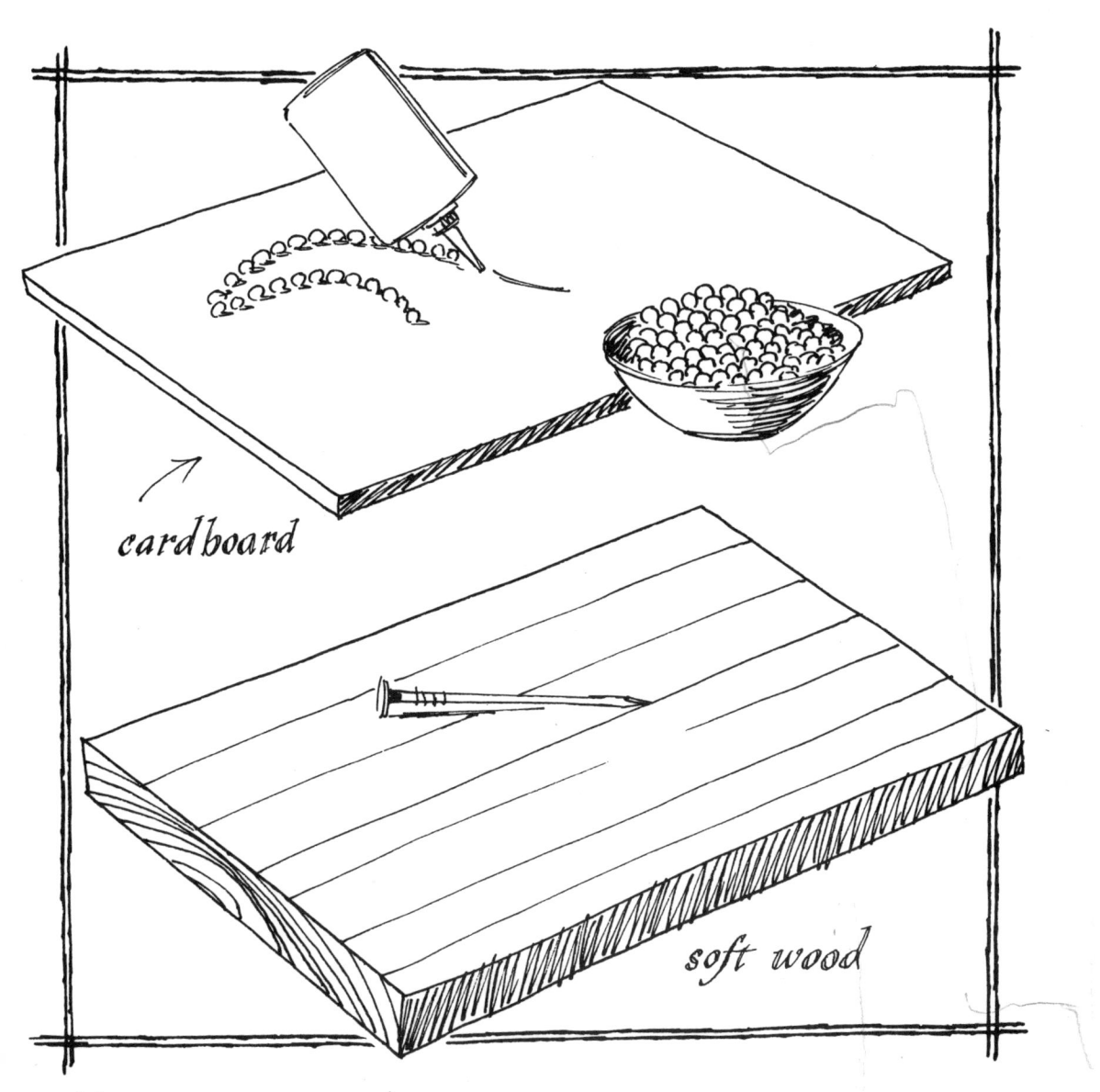

soft wood

21

Tools and materials

You will need some special materials to make your block prints. You can purchase some of them at a hobby store, and you will have some of them around your house. You will need:

a tube of water-base block printing ink

newsprint paper, construction paper, or, after you learn how to make especially clear prints, a more expensive paper like rice paper

a rubber brayer (A brayer is sometimes called an ink roller, and it is used very much like the rollers people use to paint their walls.)

a wooden spoon

spray lacquer or heavy hair spray

a cookie sheet or a piece of heavy plastic.

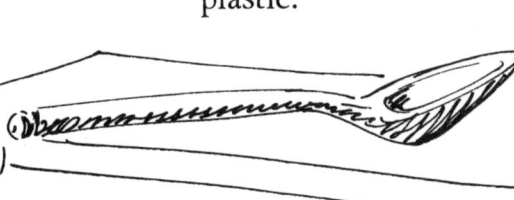

23

A bean block

Let's begin with a block with a raised surface. You can make a bean block that will print very nicely. You will need:

    a square or rectangle of cardboard
    white glue
    dried beans or peas.

First, draw a design you like on the cardboard. Would you like to make a bird? Or a flower? Or a design with circles and triangles? Make the design simple. A simple design will make a clearer print.

When you have finished your drawing, fill it in by gluing the beans or peas to the cardboard. Remember that the beans or peas that you glue on will be the parts of the block that will print. Do not glue the beans where you want to have a blank space. Let the plate dry thoroughly when you have finished gluing—at least overnight.

cardboard

white glue

peas or beans

remember that the beans or peas you glue on will be the parts that print

After the plate is dry, you can begin to make prints with it. Cover the table you work on with newspapers as you did to make the vegetable prints. You need a paper cushion for block prints too. Put a layer of paper towels on top of the newspapers. Place the bean plate on top of the paper towels.

Squeeze about one inch of ink from the tube onto the cookie sheet or piece of plastic. Roll the ink brayer back and forth through the ink until the brayer is coated with ink.

Then roll the brayer back and forth over the plate. You may need to roll the brayer in the ink again. Continue to roll the inked brayer over the plate until the beans are completely covered with ink.

Now you can make a print. Place a sheet of paper on top of the inked bean block. It does not matter if the paper is larger than the plate. When you have finished your print, the extra paper will make a nice border for the print.

Hold the paper in place on top of the block with one hand, and rub the paper with the wooden spoon or with your fingers. Rub gently so that you do not tear the paper, but be sure that the paper touches all of the places where the beans are glued. Try to rub evenly too. If you do not rub evenly, the finished print will look lighter in some spots and darker in others.

Peel the paper away from the block very carefully. At this point, a French boy or girl would say, "Voila!" You have made a new kind of print! Perhaps your first print is smudged or uneven. Try again. You can make many prints from your bean block.

paper 4.

inked block

wooden spoon 5.

6.

peel paper away carefully

lace
burlap
corduroy

abstract design

spray several times

A fabric block

Would you like to make a block with different kinds of cloth? Again, you should begin with a square or rectangle of cardboard. You can use many kinds of cloth on the same block. Use heavy lace, or corduroy, or burlap, or nylon net.

Spread a thin layer of glue over the entire cardboard. Then glue the pieces of fabric onto the cardboard to form a design. This time you may not want to make a design that looks like an object you recognize. This kind of design is called an "abstract" design. But be sure that all of the edges of the cloth are glued firmly. When the glue has thoroughly dried, spray the block several times with hair spray. Make prints with the fabric block just as you did with the bean block.

A wood block

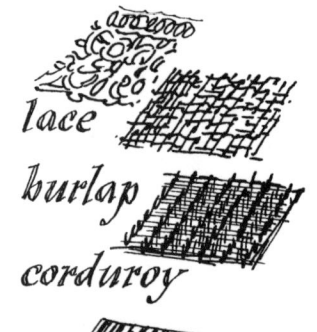

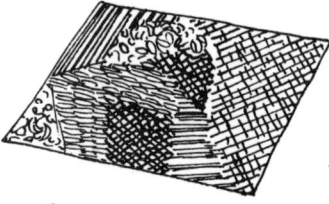

Let's make a block that has a design scratched and pounded into it. This block is different from the bean block and the fabric block. The surface of this block will print and the scratches and dents will be blank. You will need:

    a hammer

    a nail

    screws and nuts from the tool chest

    a piece of window screen

    a square or rectangle of *soft* wood like pine.

Draw a design on the wood with the nail as you would with a pencil. Press hard with the nail so that you make deep lines in the wood. Add interest to your design by making dents with the screws, nuts, and window screen. Place one of these objects at a time on the wood and pound it hard several times with the hammer. The dents must be quite deep. When you remove the object, you will see the mark that it has made in the wood. You can print with this plate as soon as you have finished your design.

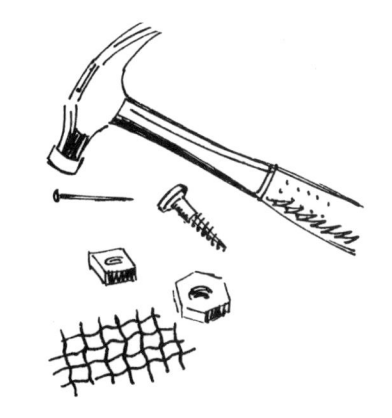

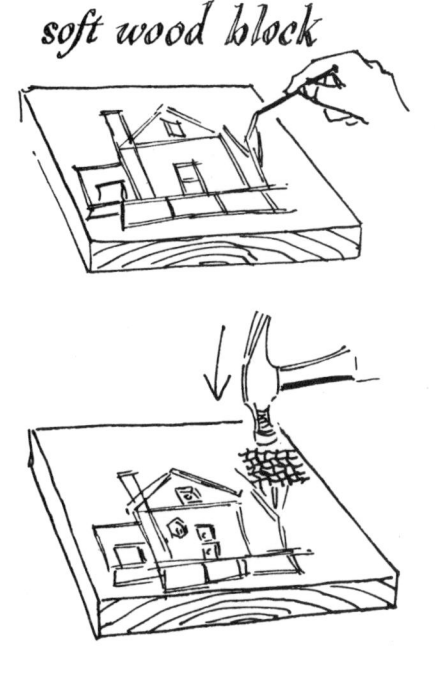

soft wood block

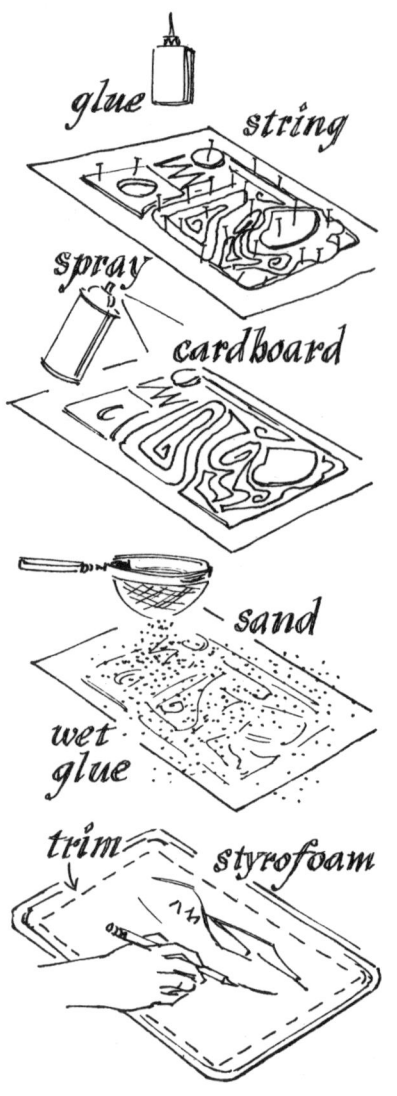

Other projects

You can make many kinds of raised or indented blocks. You can glue pieces of cardboard and string onto a cardboard surface in a design you like. Pin the string with common (or straight) pins placed one inch apart until the glue dries. Then remove the pins and spray the block with lacquer. Let it dry thoroughly.

Spread glue on a cardboard surface in the form of a design, and then sprinkle sand on the cardboard. The sand will stick to the places where glue has been applied. Shake the extra sand off gently, dry the block overnight, and make your prints.

Make a block like the wood block with a styrofoam meat tray from the supermarket. Cut the sides from the meat tray, and you will have a flat piece of styrofoam. Use the smooth side of the meat tray and draw a design you like with a pencil. Make the lines deep, but use a dull pencil. A sharp pencil might tear the styrofoam.

Make prints with the meat tray block as you did with the wood block.

Make a raised plate or a wood plate with letters on it. You might want to print your name or initials, or a slogan like "Love" or "Peace." Glue string on cardboard or scratch the letters into wood. But you should make a mirror image of the letters so that you can read them when your print is finished. My name is Suellen. This is how I would write it on a block print:
If you make a small block with your initials on it, you can stamp it on all of your treasures. Then you can always identify your own books, records, and toys.

a mirror image

When you have finished printing for the day, you should clean up your work area. Throw out the newspapers. Wash all of your tools with warm water. Wipe your blocks clean with a damp cloth.

Before you wash your hands, make some fingerprints on a piece of paper. Add a few lines with a pencil or pen. See what you can make with a fingerprint!